Alina's Story

Writers of the Round Table Press
PO Box 511
Highland Park, IL 60035

Number 4
in the series:
The ORP Library

Story Adaptation	SHANE CLESTER
Illustration	SHANE CLESTER
Publisher	COREY MICHAEL BLAKE
Executive Editor	KATIE GUTIERREZ
Post Production	DAVID CHARLES COHEN
Directoress of Happiness	ERIN COHEN
Director of Author Services	KRISTIN WESTBERG
Facts Keeper	MIKE WINICOUR
Front Cover Design	SHANE CLESTER, SUNNY DIMARTINO
Interior Design and Layout	SUNNY DIMARTINO
Proofreading	RITA HESS
Last Looks	JESS PLACE
Digital Book Conversion	SUNNY DIMARTINO
Digital Publishing	SUNNY DIMARTINO

Printed in the United States of America

First Edition: March 2013
10 9 8 7 6 5 4 3 2

Library of Congress Cataloging-in-Publication Data
Krukar, Jeff
Alina's story: learning how to trust, heal, and hope / Jeff Krukar and Katie Gutierrez
with James G. Balestrieri.—1st ed. p. cm.
Print ISBN: 978-1-939418-18-0   Digital ISBN: 978-1-939418-17-3
Library of Congress Control Number: 2013935856
The ORP Library: Alina's Story

RTC Publishing is an imprint of Writers of the Round Table, Inc.
Writers of the Round Table Press and the RTC Publishing logo
are trademarks of Writers of the Round Table, Inc.

Alina's Story

LEARNING HOW TO TRUST, HEAL, AND HOPE

THE ORP LIBRARY

ADAPTED AND
ILLUSTRATED BY
SHANE CLESTER

WRITTEN
BY
WITH

JEFF KRUKAR, PH.D.
KATIE GUTIERREZ
JAMES G. BALESTRIERI

INTRODUCTION

I have led Oconomowoc Residential Programs (ORP) for almost thirty years. We're a family of companies offering specialized services and care for children, adolescents, and adults with disabilities. Too often, when parents of children with disabilities try to find funding for programs like ours, they are bombarded by red tape, conflicting information, or no information at all, so they struggle blindly for years to secure an appropriate education. Meanwhile, home life, and the child's wellbeing, suffers. In cases when parents and caretakers have exhausted their options—and their hope—ORP is here to help. We felt it was time to offer parents a new, unexpected tool to fight back: stories that educate, empower, and inspire.

The original idea was to create a library of comic books that could empower families with information to re-claim their rights. We wanted to give parents and care-takers the information they need to advocate for themselves, as well as provide educators and therapists with a therapeutic tool. And, of course, we wanted to reach the children—to offer them a visual representa-tion of their journey that would show that they aren't alone, nor are they wrong or "bad" for their differences.

What we found in the process of writing original stories for the comics is that these journeys are too long, too complex, to be contained within a standard comic. So what we are now creating is an ORP library of disabilities books—traditional books geared toward parents, care-takers, educators, and therapists, *and* comic books like this one that portray the world through the eyes of children with disabilities. Both styles of books share what we have learned while advocating for families over the years while also honestly highlighting their emotional journeys.

In an ideal situation, this companion children's book will be used therapeutically, to communicate directly with these amazing children, and to help support the work ORP and companies like ours are doing. These books are the best I have to offer and if they even help a handful of people the effort will have been worth it.

Sincerely,

Jim Balestrieri
CEO, Oconomowoc Residential Programs

A NOTE ABOUT THIS BOOK

Complex trauma and reactive attachment disorder are conditions that affect children in different ways. The child depicted in the following story struggles with significant emotional and behavioral difficulties that require short-term placement in a specialized therapeutic environment. Many children with complex trauma do not resemble the child shown in this story. However, those who are similar to Alina face challenges that make it difficult to benefit from special education in a traditional public school setting. Genesee Lake School strives to build relationships with the children in its care so that they learn new skills that will lead to a successful transition back to their homes, schools, and communities. It is our hope that the following story will add to your own understanding of the often lonely journey experienced by families with children with these unique challenges and gifts.

Alina's

Story

ALINA WAS A LITTLE GIRL WHO LIVED
IN AN ORPHANAGE IN RUSSIA.

LIVING IN THE ORPHANAGE
WAS VERY HARD FOR ALINA.

MAMA

PAPA

ONE DAY, A FAMILY
CAME FROM AMERICA
TO ADOPT ALINA.

ALINA

BROTHER

RUSSIA

ALINA'S NEW MAMA AND PAPA
LOVED HER VERY MUCH AND WERE
EXCITED TO BRING HER HOME.

AMERICA

ALINA HAD SPENT HER WHOLE LIFE IN THE ORPHANAGE. SHE WAS FRIGHTENED AND CONFUSED BY MANY THINGS IN THE OUTSIDE WORLD.

WHEN SHE WAS SCARED, WORRIED, OR UNCERTAIN, ALINA THREW BIG TANTRUMS.

SOMETIMES SHE JUST FROZE; BUT MOST OFTEN SHE SCREAMED, HIT, OR TRIED TO RUN AWAY.

EVERYONE IN THE FAMILY WAS EXCITED TO MEET ALINA. AUNTS, UNCLES, GRANDMAS, AND GRANDPAS ALL CAME TO WELCOME HER. IT WAS A LITTLE OVERWHELMING!

ALINA HAD HER OWN ROOM IN THE NEW HOUSE. ALINA'S NEW BROTHER HAD HIS OWN ROOM, TOO, AND SO DID MAMA AND PAPA.

BUT ALINA LIKED FOR MAMA TO SLEEP WITH HER. SHE WORRIED WHETHER HER ROOM REALLY BELONGED TO HER, WHETHER THERE WOULD BE FOOD TO EAT IN THE MORNING, AND IF MAMA WOULD STILL BE THERE WHEN SHE WOKE.

WHEN IT WAS TIME FOR BED, MAMA TRIED TO BRUSH ALINA'S HAIR AND GIVE HER A BATH. ALINA'S MAMA LOVED HER AND JUST WANTED TO TAKE CARE OF HER. ALINA DID NOT UNDERSTAND. SHE HAD NEVER EXPERIENCED THIS MUCH AFFECTION OR CLOSENESS BEFORE.

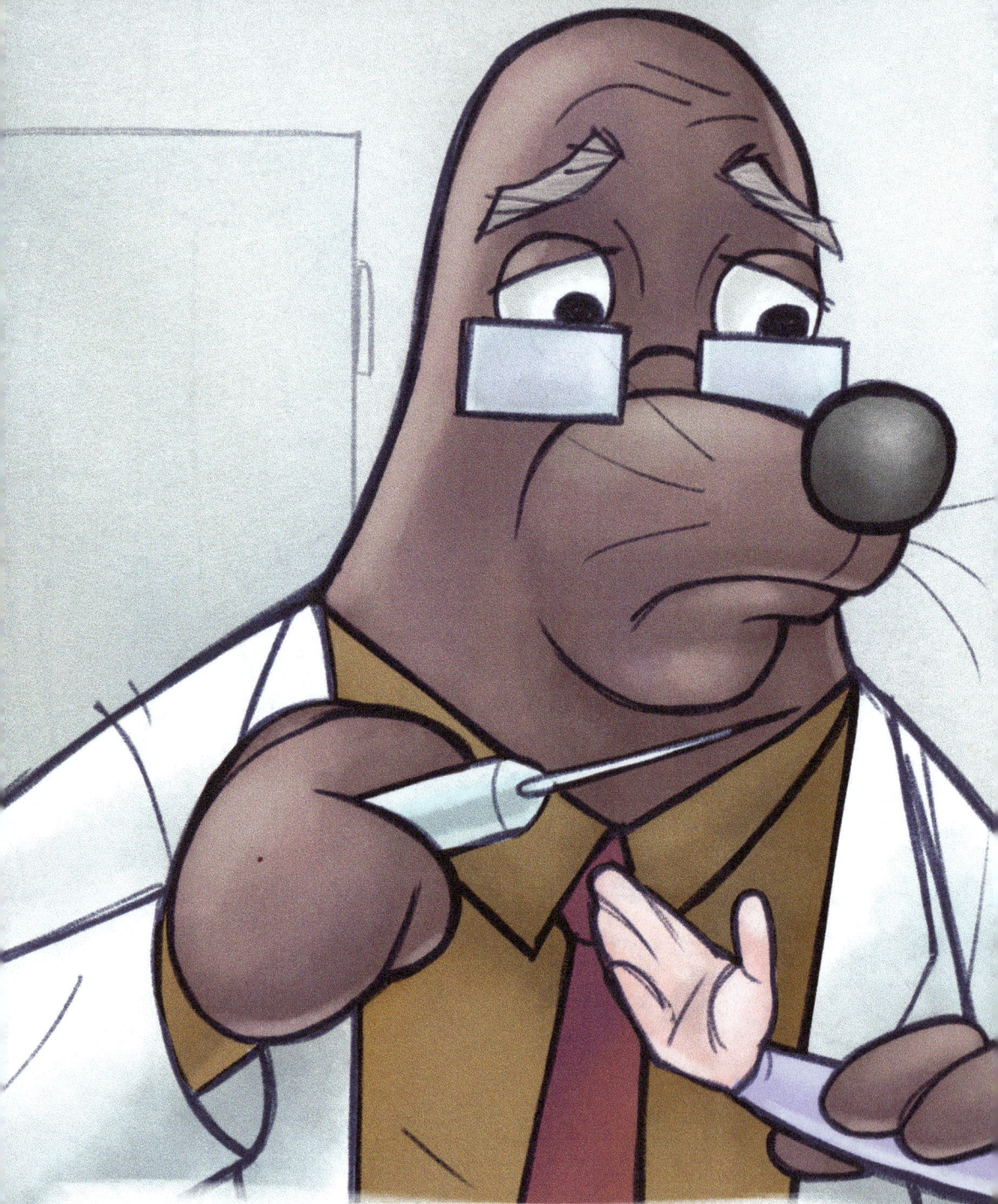

SINCE ALINA CAME FROM FAR AWAY, MAMA AND PAPA TOOK HER TO THE DOCTOR FOR A CHECK-UP. ALINA HAD TO GET A SHOT. SHE WAS SCARED AND DID NOT LIKE SHOTS!

ALINA HAD A HARD TIME TALKING ABOUT HER FEELINGS. SHE DIDN'T LIKE CHANGES, WHEN SHE WAS TOLD "NO," OR WHEN IT WAS TIME TO STOP DOING SOMETHING SHE ENJOYED.

FUN TIMES COULD QUICKLY TURN INTO BAD TIMES.

ALINA! TIME TO COME INSIDE, PLEASE!

MAMA AND PAPA WERE VERY WORRIED ABOUT ALINA. THEY DIDN'T KNOW WHY SHE SCREAMED AND HIT, AND THEY DIDN'T WANT HER TO HURT HERSELF OR SOMEONE ELSE. THE NEXT DAY, THEY TOOK ALINA TO A DOCTOR TO SEE IF HE COULD HELP.

THE DOCTOR WANTED ALINA TO STAY OVERNIGHT AT THE HOSPITAL SO HE COULD WATCH HER AND MAKE SURE SHE WAS OKAY.

ALINA'S PARENTS WERE SAD TO LEAVE HER AT THE HOSPITAL, BUT IF THE DOCTOR COULD HELP HER, LETTING ALINA STAY OVERNIGHT WAS THE BEST CHOICE.

THE DOCTOR ASKED ALINA QUESTIONS.
THEN ALINA DREW PICTURES WITH HIM.
HE WANTED TO SEE HER DRAW A HOUSE
AND A FAMILY, BUT ALINA DIDN'T DRAW
ANYTHING. SHE DIDN'T KNOW WHAT
"FAMILY" MEANT.

AFTER THE HOSPITAL, ALINA'S PARENTS AND THE DOCTOR WORKED TOGETHER TO MAKE A PLAN FOR ALINA — A SPECIAL PLAN TO HELP HER AS SHE STARTED SCHOOL.

ALINA LIKED SCHOOL AND HER TEACHER BUT HAD A HARD TIME ADJUSTING. SHE DIDN'T KNOW HOW TO MAKE FRIENDS AND OFTEN REFUSED TO DO THINGS SHE DIDN'T WANT TO DO.

YEARS PASSED, AND ALINA STILL COULD NOT TALK ABOUT HER FEELINGS. IT WAS HARD FOR HER TO TRUST OTHER PEOPLE. NO MATTER WHAT MAMA, PAPA, TEACHERS, AND DOCTORS TRIED, AS ALINA GOT BIGGER SO DID HER TANTRUMS. SHE WAS TRYING TO TELL PEOPLE WHAT SHE THOUGHT AND FELT BUT DIDN'T KNOW HOW.

THEN ONE DAY AT DINNER, THINGS GOT REALLY BAD. PAPA TRIED TO CLEAR AWAY ALINA'S PLATE. ALINA WASN'T DONE AND PANICKED. SHE GRABBED A KNIFE...

SHE SCARED HER MAMA AND PAPA, BUT THANKFULLY SHE DIDN'T HURT THEM OR HERSELF TOO BADLY. STILL, ALINA HAD TO GO TO THE HOSPITAL AGAIN.

AFTER THE HOSPITAL, MAMA AND PAPA
KNEW THAT THEY NEEDED MORE HELP.
MAMA HAD HEARD ABOUT A SPECIAL SCHOOL
WHERE KIDS LIKE ALINA WENT TO LIVE FOR
A WHILE TO LEARN NEW SKILLS, AND THEY
HOPED THE SCHOOL COULD HELP.

GENESEE
LAKE
SCHOOL

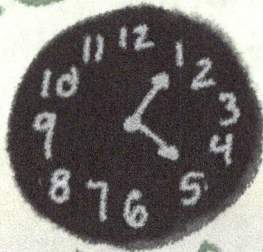

EVEN THOUGH MAMA AND PAPA WOULD MISS ALINA VERY MUCH, THEY DECIDED TO LET HER GO TO THE NEW SCHOOL TO LEARN HOW TO EXPRESS HER FEELINGS AND SOLVE PROBLEMS.

ALINA WOULD BE
LIVING AT THE
SCHOOL FOR A WHILE.
EVERYONE WAS SAD
TO SAY GOODBYE.

THE STAFF AT THE SCHOOL WERE ALWAYS THERE TO HELP ALINA. MELANIE WAS ONE OF THEM. SHE SPENT LOTS OF TIME WITH ALINA AND TALKED TO MAMA AND PAPA A LOT ON THE PHONE. WHEN ALINA WAS SCARED TO GO TO SCHOOL, MELANIE HELPED HER FIGURE OUT THAT HAVING A PICTURE OF HER PARENTS TAPED INSIDE HER NOTEBOOK MADE HER FEEL BETTER.

OR WHEN ALINA WORRIED THE FOOD WAS GOING TO RUN OUT AND TRIED TO FIGHT HER WAY TO THE FRONT OF THE LINE, MELANIE HELPED HER REALIZE WHY SHE GOT SO UPSET.

I'M AFRAID THERE'S NOT ENOUGH FOOD FOR ME TO EAT TOO.

WE WON'T RUN OUT OF FOOD, THERE'S ENOUGH FOR EVERYONE. SEE?

ALINA LEARNED HOW TO EXPRESS HERSELF, SHARE HER FEELINGS, AND SOLVE PROBLEMS.

AS MUCH AS ALINA WAS LEARNING
AND GROWING AT HER NEW SCHOOL,
SHE STILL DIDN'T WANT TO GET OUT
OF BED IN THE MORNING!

TIME TO
GET UP,
ALINA!

NO!

CAN I TALK TO YOU FOR A FEW MINUTES?
YES...
WE'VE SEEN IT'S NOT GOING WELL FOR YOU AT WAKE-UP TIME.
WHAT'S HAPPENING?
IT'S COLD IN THE MORNING WHEN I GET DRESSED.

OH, OK. I UNDERSTAND THAT. THE THING IS WHEN THIS HAPPENS YOU'VE BEEN LATE FOR SCHOOL. I WONDER IF THERE IS A WAY THAT YOU CAN FEEL WARMER IN THE MORNING AT WAKE-UP AND STILL BE AT SCHOOL ON TIME. DO YOU HAVE ANY IDEAS?
NO.
WOULD IT HELP IF YOU LAID OUT YOUR CLOTHES THE NIGHT BEFORE AND GOT DRESSED UNDER THE COVERS?
I THINK SO...

WHEN ALINA'S FAMILY VISITED, THEY WERE SO PROUD OF ALINA! ALINA WAS LEARNING A LOT AND SEEMED HAPPIER.

ALINA HAD COME SO FAR THAT SHE WAS GOING ON OVERNIGHT TRIPS WITH HER FAMILY.

ONE MORNING, THEY LEARNED ALINA WOULD SOON BE MOVING INTO A GROUP HOME, WHERE SHE WOULD HAVE MORE INDEPENDENCE AND RESPONSIBILITIES. IT WAS A BIG STEP!

HaPPY :)

HOW THESE BOOKS
WERE CREATED

The ORP Library of disabilities books is the result of heartfelt collaboration between numerous people: the staff of ORP, including the CEO, executive director, psychologists, clinical coordinators, teachers, and more; the families of children with disabilities served by ORP, including some of the children themselves; and the Round Table Companies (RTC) storytelling team. To create these books, RTC conducted dozens of intensive, intimate interviews over a period of months and performed independent research in order to truthfully and accurately depict the lives of these families. We are grateful to all those who donated their time in support of this message, generously sharing their experience, wisdom, and—most importantly—their stories so that the books will ring true. While each story is fictional and not based on any one family or child, we could not have envisioned the world through their eyes without the access we were so lovingly given. It is our hope that in reading this uniquely personal book, you felt the spirit of everyone who contributed to its creation.

ACKNOWLEDGMENTS

The authors would like to thank the following team members at Genesee Lake School and ORP who generously lent their time and expertise to this book: special education teacher Jade Gorecki, licensed psychologist Anne Felden, and clinical coordinator Christy Lynch. Your passion, experience, and wisdom make this book an invaluable tool for other educators, families, and therapists. Thank you for your enthusiastic contributions to this project.

We would also like to extend our deepest gratitude to the families who invited us into their worlds (and, in some cases, their homes!). Chris and Heidi Burrows, Lori and Karl Hetzel (and Logan, Connor Dane, Delaney, and Nadya), and Marilyn Tauscher—the courage, ferocity, and love with which you shepherd your children through their lives is nothing short of heroic. Thank you for sharing your journeys with us, from the joy of adoption to the fear of the unknown to the hope for the future. You are the reason we are telling this story—and the only reason we could do so authentically.

And to readers of *Alina's Story*—the parents committed to helping their children, the educators who teach those children skills needed for greater independence, the therapists who shine a light on what can be a frighteningly mysterious road, and the schools and counties that make difficult financial decisions to benefit these children: thank you. Your work is miraculous.

RESOURCES

Allen, Jeffrey S., and Roger J. Klein. *Ready . . . Set . . . R.E.L.A.X.: A Research Based Program of Relaxation, Learning, and Self-Esteem for Children*. Watertown, WI: Inner Coaching, 1996.

American Association of Children's Residential Centers. *Redefining Residential: Trauma-Informed Care in Residential Treatment*. Position Paper. Milwaukee, WI: American Association of Children's Residential Centers, 2010.

American Psychiatric Association. *Diagnostic and Statistical Manual of Mental Disorders, Fourth Edition, Text Revision*. Washington, DC: American Psychiatric Association, 2000.

Blaustein, Margaret E., and Kristine M. Kinniburgh. *Treating Traumatic Stress in Children and Adolescents: How to Foster Resilience through Attachment, Self-Regulation, and Competency*. New York: The Guilford Press, 2010.

Buron, Kari D., and Mitzi Curtis. *The Incredible 5-point Scale: Assisting Students with Autism Spectrum Disorders in Understanding Social interactions and Controlling Their Emotional Responses*. Shawnee Mission, KS: Autism Asperger Publishing Co., 2003.

Greene, Ross W. *The Explosive Child*. New York: Harper Collins Publishers, 2005.

Greene, Ross W., and J. Stuart Ablon. *Treating Explosive Kids: The Collaborative Problem-Solving Approach*. New York: The Guilford Press, 2006.

Greenspan, Stanley, and Serena Wiedera. *The Child with Special Needs: Encouraging Intellectual and Emotional Growth.* Cambridge, MA: Da Capo Press, 1998.

IDEA – Building the Legacy: IDEA 2004, *http://idea.ed.gov.*

Interdisciplinary Council on Developmental and Learning Disorders, *http://www.icdl.com.*

Massachusetts Department of Mental Health "Restraint/Seclusion Reduction Initiative: Safety Tool," *http://www.mass.gov/dmh/rsri.*

Siegel, Daniel J., and Tina Payne Bryson. *The Whole Brain Child: 12 Revolutionary Strategies to Nurture Your Child's Developing Mind.* New York: Delacorte Press, 2011.

Smith Myles, Brenda, and Jack Southwick. *Asperger Syndrome and Difficult Moments: Practical Solutions for Tantrums, Rage, and Meltdowns.* Shawnee Mission, KS: Autism Asperger Publishing Co., 2005.

Think:Kids, Rethinking Challenging Kids, *http://www.thinkkids.org.*

van der Kolk, Bessel A. "Developmental Trauma Disorder: Toward a Rational Diagnosis for Children with Complex Trauma Histories." *Psychiatric Annals,* 35 (2005): 401–408.

SHANE CLESTER

BIOGRAPHY

As a child, **Shane Clester** loved drawing. Robots, ninjas, He-Man figures, lyrics from Lionel Ritchie songs; Shane drew everything. He was either going to be an astronaut or an artist when he grew up, or a ninja robot fighting astronaut. Finding out later that he didn't have the eyesight to be an astronaut, and that a ninja robot fighting astronaut wasn't a real thing, he pursued his art. He worked a virtual cornucopia of odd jobs before becoming a professional doodle monkey. Shane has had a varied and fulfilling career so far, is drawing his 10th for Round Table Companies, and looks forward to the day when, as an old man, he looks out the window of his moon base reflecting back on his life. But for now, Shane lives in sunny southern Florida with his cutie pie wife, snuggly pets, and reasonably sized action figure collection; hoping each time that his next leap will be his leap home.

Shane would like to dedicate this book to Chris, Jesse, Mike, and all the Hazelton boys.

JEFFREY D. KRUKAR, PH.D.

BIOGRAPHY

Jeffrey D. Krukar, Ph.D. is a licensed psychologist and certified school psychologist with more than 20 years of experience working with children and families in a variety of settings, including community based group homes, vocational rehabilitation services, residential treatment, juvenile corrections, public schools, and private practice. He earned his Ph.D. in educational psychology, with a school psychology specialization and psychology minor, from the University of Wisconsin-Milwaukee. Dr. Krukar is a registrant of the National Register of Health Service Providers in Psychology, and is also a member of the American Psychological Association.

As the psychologist at Genesee Lake School in Oconomowoc, WI, Dr. Krukar believes it truly takes a village to raise a child—to strengthen developmental foundations in relating, communicating, and thinking—so they can successfully return to their families and communities. Dr. Krukar hopes the ORP Library of disabilities books will bring to light the stories of children and families to a world that is generally not aware of their challenges and successes, as well as offer a sense of hope to those currently on this journey. His deepest hope is that some of the concepts in these books resonate with parents and professionals working with kids with disabilities, and offer possibilities that will help kids achieve their maximum potential and life enjoyment.

KATIE GUTIERREZ

BIOGRAPHY

Katie Gutierrez believes that a well-told story can transcend what a reader "knows" to be real about the world—and thus change the world for that reader. In every form, story is transformative, and Katie is proud to spend her days immersed in it as executive editor for Round Table Companies, Inc.

Since 2007, Katie has edited approximately 50 books and co-written six—including *Meltdown*, one of the ORP Library of disabilities books. She has been humbled by the stories she has heard and hopes these books will help guide families on their often-lonely journeys, connecting them with resources and support. She also hopes they will give the general population a glimpse into the Herculean jobs taken on so fiercely by parents, doctors, therapists, educators, and others who live with, work with, and love children such as Alina.

Katie holds a BA in English and philosophy from Southwestern University and an MFA in fiction from Texas State University. She has contributed to or been profiled in publications including *Forbes*, *Entrepreneur* magazine, *People* magazine, *Hispanic Executive Quarterly*, and *Narrative* magazine. She can't believe she's lucky enough to do what she loves every day.

JAMES G. BALESTRIERI

BIOGRAPHY

James G. Balestrieri is currently the CEO of Oconomowoc Residential Programs, Inc. (ORP). He has worked in the human services field for 40 years, holding positions that run the gamut to include assistant maintenance, assistant cook, direct care worker, teacher's aide, summer camp counselor, bookkeeper, business administrator, marketing director, CFO, and CEO. Jim graduated from Marquette University with a B.S. in Business Administration (1977) and a Master's in Business Administration with an emphasis in Marketing (1988). He is also a Certified Public Accountant (Wisconsin—1982). Jim has a passion for creatively addressing the needs of those with impairments by managing the inherent stress among funding, programming, and profitability. He believes that those with a disability enjoy rights and protections that were created by the hard-fought efforts of those who came before them; that the Civil Rights movement is not just for minority groups; and that people with disabilities have a right to find their place in the world and to achieve their maximum potential as individuals. For more information, see *www.orp.com*.

ABOUT ORP

Oconomowoc Residential Programs, Inc. is an employee-owned family of companies whose mission is to make a difference in the lives of people with disabilities. Our dedicated staff of 2,000 employee owners provides quality services and professional care to more than 1,700 children, adolescents, and adults with special needs. ORP provides a continuum of care, including residential therapeutic education, community-based residential services, support services, respite care, treatment programs, and day services. The individuals in our care include people with developmental disabilities, physical disabilities, and intellectual disabilities. **Our guiding principle is passion:** a passion for the people we serve and for the work we do. For a comprehensive look at our programs and people, please visit *www.orp.com.*

ORP offers two residential therapeutic education programs and one alternative day school among its array of services. These programs offer developmentally appropriate education and treatment for children, adolescents, and young adults in settings specially attuned to their needs. We provide special programs for students with specific academic and social issues relative to a wide range of disabilities, including autistic disorder, Asperger's disorder, mental retardation, anxiety disorders, depression, bipolar disorder, reactive attachment disorder, attention deficit disorder, Prader-Willi Syndrome, and other disabilities.

Genesee Lake School is a nationally recognized provider of comprehensive residential treatment, educational, and vocational services for children, adolescents, and young adults with emotional, mental health, neurological, or developmental disabilities. GLS has specific expertise in Autism Spectrum Disorders, anxiety and mood disorders, and behavioral disorders. We provide an individualized, person-centered, integrated team approach, which emphasizes positive behavioral support, therapeutic relationships, and developmentally appropriate practices. Our goal is to assist each individual to acquire skills to live, learn, and succeed in a community-based, less restrictive environment. GLS is particularly known for its high quality educational services for residential and day school students.

Genesee Lake School / Admissions Director
36100 Genesee Lake Road
Oconomowoc, WI 53066
262-569-5510
http://www.geneseelakeschool.com

T.C. Harris School is located in an attractive setting in Lafayette, Indiana. T.C. Harris teaches skills to last a lifetime, through a full therapeutic program as well as day school and other services.

T.C. Harris School / Admissions Director
3700 Rome Drive
Lafayette, IN 47905
765-448-4220
http://tcharrisschool.com

The Richardson School is a day school in West Allis, Wisconsin that provides an effective, positive alternative education environment serving children from Milwaukee and the surrounding communities.

The Richardson School / Director
6753 West Roger Street
West Allis, WI 53219
414-540-8500
http://www.richardsonschool.com

REACTIVE ATTACHMENT DISORDER

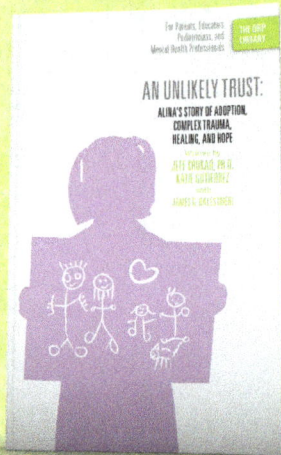

AN UNLIKELY TRUST
ALINA'S STORY OF ADOPTION, COMPLEX TRAUMA, HEALING, AND HOPE

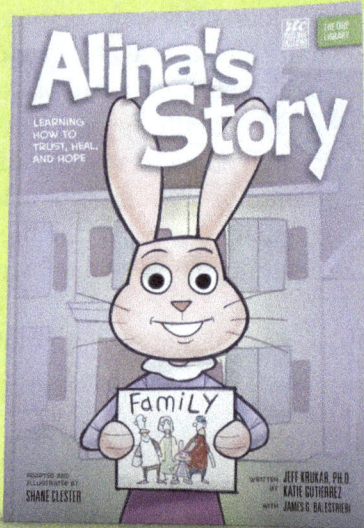

ALINA'S STORY
LEARNING HOW TO TRUST, HEAL, AND HOPE

An Unlikely Trust: Alina's Story of Adoption, Complex Trauma, Healing, and Hope, and its companion children's book, *Alina's Story*, share the journey of Alina, a young girl adopted from Russia. After living in an orphanage during her early life, Alina is unequipped to cope with the complexities of the outside world. She has a deep mistrust of others and finds it difficult to talk about her feelings. When she is frightened, overwhelmed, or confused, she lashes out in rages that scare her family. Alina's parents know she needs help and work endlessly to find it for her, eventually discovering a special school that will teach Alina new skills. Slowly, Alina gets better at expressing her feelings and solving problems. For the first time in her life, she realizes she is truly safe and loved . . . and capable of loving in return.

ASPERGER'S DISORDER

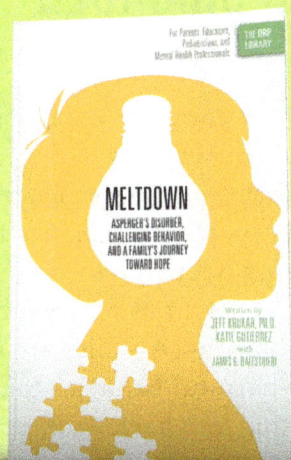

MELTDOWN
ASPERGER'S DISORDER, CHALLENGING BEHAVIOR, AND A FAMILY'S JOURNEY TOWARD HOPE

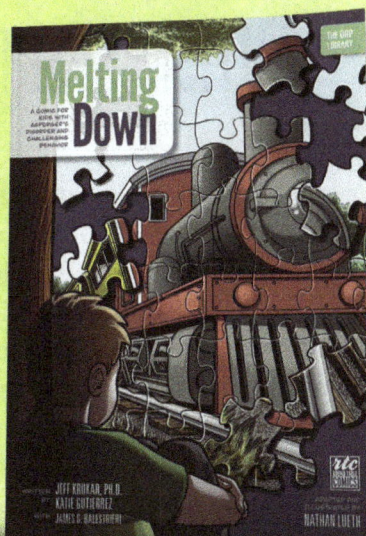

MELTING DOWN
A COMIC FOR KIDS WITH ASPERGER'S DISORDER AND CHALLENGING BEHAVIOR

Meltdown and its companion comic book, *Melting Down*, are both based on the fictional story of Benjamin, a boy diagnosed with Asperger's disorder and additional challenging behavior. From the time Benjamin is a toddler, he and his parents know he is different: he doesn't play with his sister, refuses to make eye contact, and doesn't communicate well with others. And his tantrums are not like normal tantrums; they're meltdowns that will eventually make regular schooling—and day-to-day life—impossible. Both the prose book, intended for parents, educators, and mental health professionals, and the comic for the kids themselves demonstrate that the journey toward hope isn't simple . . . but with the right tools and teammates, it's possible.

AUTISM SPECTRUM DISORDER

Mr. Incredible shares the fictional story of Adam, a boy diagnosed with autistic disorder. On Adam's first birthday, his mother recognizes that something is different about him: he recoils from the touch of his family, preferring to accept physical contact only in the cool water of the family's pool. As Adam grows older, he avoids eye contact, is largely nonverbal, and has very specific ways of getting through the day; when those habits are disrupted, intense meltdowns and self-harmful behavior follow. From seeking a diagnosis to advocating for special education services, from keeping Adam safe to discovering his strengths, his family becomes his biggest champion. The journey to realizing Adam's potential isn't easy, but with hope, love, and the right tools and teammates, they find that Adam truly is *Mr. Incredible*. The companion comic in this series, inspired by social stories, offers an innovative, dynamic way to guide children—and parents, educators, and caregivers—through some of the daily struggles experienced by those with autism.

MR. INCREDIBLE

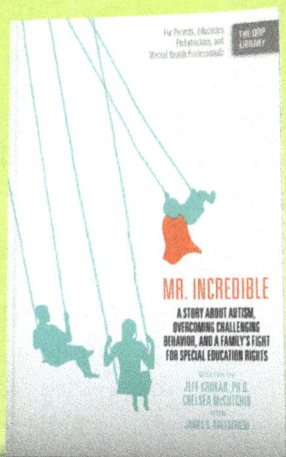

A STORY ABOUT AUTISM,
OVERCOMING CHALLENGING
BEHAVIOR, AND A FAMILY'S FIGHT
FOR SPECIAL EDUCATION RIGHTS

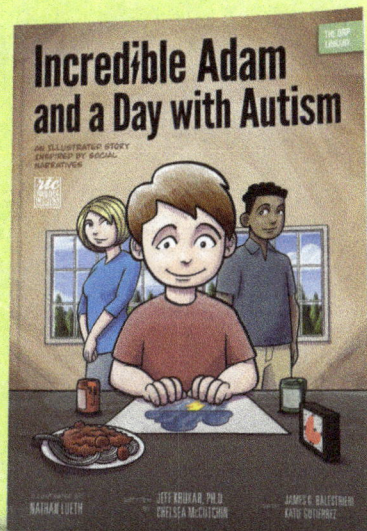

INCREDIBLE ADAM
AND A DAY WITH AUTISM

AN ILLUSTRATED STORY
INSPIRED BY SOCIAL NARRATIVES

BULLYING

Nearly one third of all school children face physical, verbal, cyber, and social bullying on a regular basis. For years, educators and parents have searched for ways to end bullying, but as that behavior becomes more sophisticated, it's harder to recognize and to stop. In *Classroom Heroes* and its companion comic book, Jason is a quiet, socially awkward seventh grade boy who has long suffered bullying in silence. While Jason's parents notice him becoming angrier and more withdrawn, they don't realize the scope of the problem until one bully takes it too far—and one teacher acts on her determination to stop it. Both *Classroom Heroes* and its companion comic recognize that in order to stop bullying, we must change our mindset. We must enlist not only parents and educators but the children themselves to create a community that simply does not tolerate bullying. Jason's story demonstrates both the heartbreaking effects of bullying and the simple yet profound strategies to end it, one student at a time.

CLASSROOM
HEROES

ONE CHILD'S STRUGGLE
WITH BULLYING AND
A TEACHER'S MISSION TO
CHANGE SCHOOL CULTURE

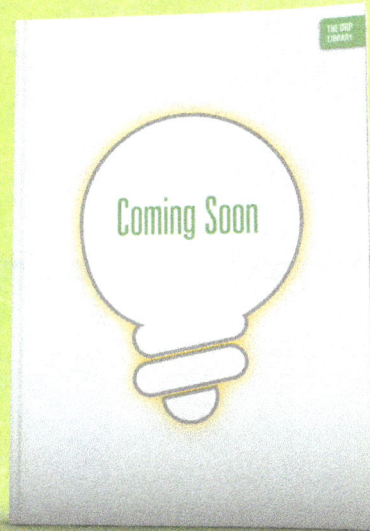

To Parents, Educators,
Pediatricians, and
Mental Health Professionals

THE ORP
LIBRARY

Written by
JEFF KRUKAR, PH.D.
PAMELA BILBRATCH
with
JAMES G. BALESTRIERI

Coming Soon

THE ORP
LIBRARY

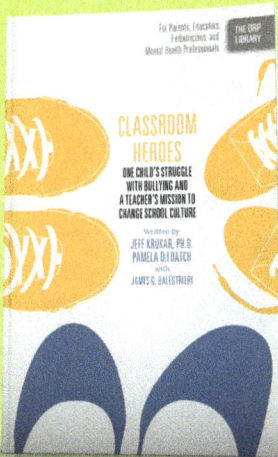

CLASSROOM HEROES
ONE CHILD'S STRUGGLE
WITH BULLYING AND
A TEACHER'S MISSION TO
CHANGE SCHOOL CULTURE

CLASSROOM HEROES
COMPANION CHILDREN'S BOOK

FAMILY SUPPORT

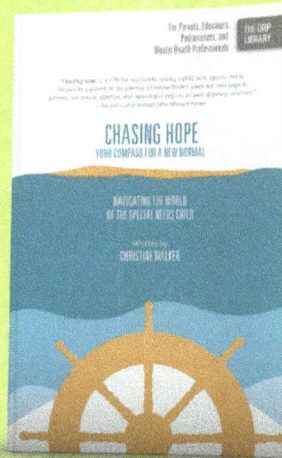

CHASING HOPE
YOUR COMPASS FOR A NEW NORMAL
NAVIGATING THE WORLD OF THE SPECIAL NEEDS CHILD

Schuyler Walker was just four years old when he was diagnosed with autism, bipolar disorder, and ADHD. In 2004, childhood mental illness was rarely talked about or understood. With knowledge and resources scarce, Schuyler's mom, Christine, navigated a lonely maze to determine what treatments, medications, and therapies could benefit her son. In the ten years since his diagnosis, Christine has often wished she had a "how to" guide that would provide the real mom-to-mom information she needed to survive the day and, in the end, help her family navigate the maze with knowledge, humor, grace, and love. Christine may not have had a manual at the beginning of her journey, but she hopes this book will serve as yours.

Also look for books on Prader-Willi Syndrome and children and psychotropic medications coming soon!

www.ingramcontent.com/pod-product-compliance
Lightning Source LLC
LaVergne TN
LVHW061221060426
835508LV00014B/1385

* 9 7 8 1 9 3 9 4 1 8 1 8 0 *